ANTS

PowerKiDS press.

New York

Suzanne Slade

To my good friend, and very hard worker, Donna Riemer

Published in 2008 by The Rosen Publishing Group, Inc.
29 East 21st Street, New York, NY 10010

First Edition

Editor: Joanne Randolph
Book Design: Julio Gil
Photo Researcher: Nicole Pristash

Photo Credits: Cover, pp. 1, 5, 7, 9, 15, 17, 19, 21 © Shutterstock.com; p. 11 © Dennis Kunkel Microscopy, Inc.; p. 13 © SuperStock, Inc.

Library of Congress Cataloging-in-Publication Data

Slade, Suzanne.
  Ants / Suzanne Slade. — 1st ed.
      p. cm. — (Under the microscope: Backyard bugs)
  Includes index.
  ISBN-13: 978-1-4042-3823-7 (library binding)
  ISBN-10: 1-4042-3823-9 (library binding)
  1. Ants—Juvenile literature. I. Title.
  QL568.F7S56 2008
  595.79'6—dc22

                                                    2007005563

Manufactured in the United States of America

Contents

Backyard Pals

It is fun to eat outside in the fresh air and sunshine. When people go on a **picnic**, they often pack food and drinks in a basket. They may sit on a blanket to eat.

If you have lunch in your backyard, you might get some surprise visitors. Ants are tiny bugs that love picnics. Most ants spend all day searching for food. Ants may take pieces of your tasty lunch back home to their family. Next time you go on a picnic, pack some extra food for the ants, your backyard pals!

Ants are very strong. They use their mouth to lift heavy food and carry it back to the nest. This red ant is out looking for food.

Home Sweet Home

Have you ever noticed a hill of dirt in your backyard? Look closely and you might see ants crawling in and out of a small hole on top of the dirt pile. This hole is the front door to an ant's home. Below the door are many rooms you cannot see.

Ants dig holes underground to make a nest. They dig tunnels between the rooms to make the nest bigger. A large group of ants living together in one nest is called a colony. Not all ants live underground. Some colonies live in pieces of dead wood or old leaves.

This ant pokes its head out of its nest. Ants have lived on Earth for over 100 million years.

Working Together

Every ant in a colony has a job to do. The queen is the most important ant. Her job is to lay eggs. The females, or girls, born without wings are the worker ants. Workers do all the work in a colony. They hunt for food, build the nest, and care for the young. The biggest workers are called soldiers. They keep the colony safe from enemies.

Male, or boy, ants and queens are born with wings. Male ants have only one job. They **mate** with a young queen. The queen then flies away to start a new colony.

There are more than 15,000 different kinds of ants living in the world. This is a bull ant, which is known to be quick to give a painful bite to keep its home safe.

Busy Body

An ant's body has three main parts, like all **insects**. They are the head, **thorax**, and **abdomen**. The head has two **compound eyes** and two long **antennae**. An ant smells with its antennae. It also uses them to feel its way through dark tunnels. An ant has strong mouthparts called mandibles. It chews food and carries heavy loads with these.

The thorax is the middle part of the body. An ant has six legs on its thorax. The abdomen is the back part of the body. This is where an ant breaks down its food. A hard **exoskeleton** covers an ant's whole body.

This close-up photo of an ant was taken with a special tool, called a scanning electron microscope. Note the ant's large mandibles.

10

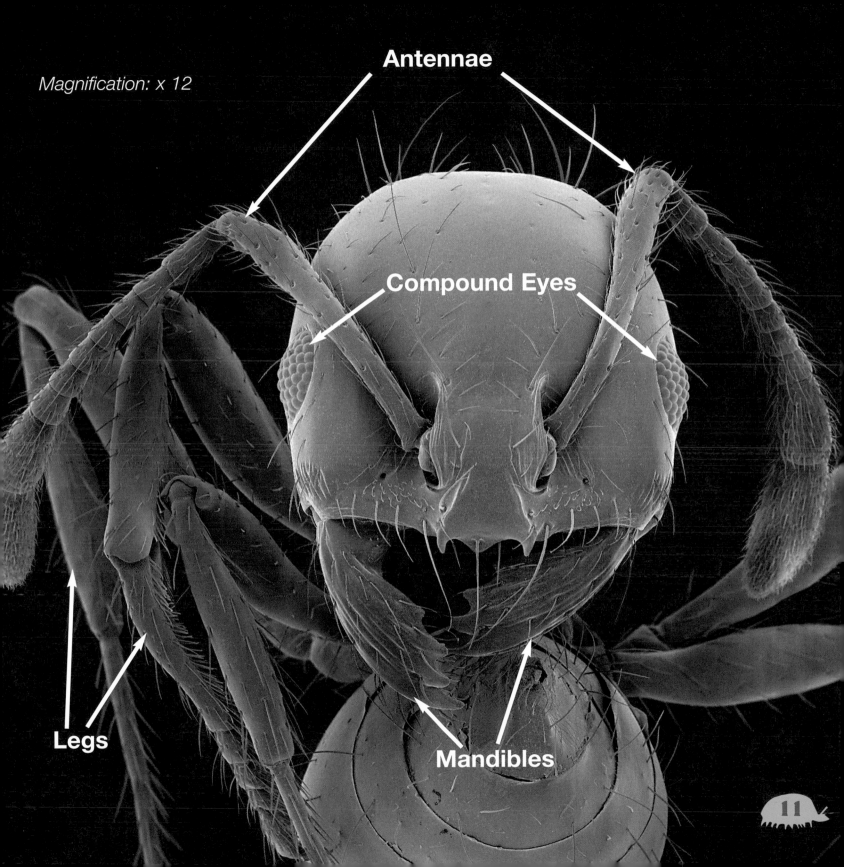

Magnification: x 12

Antennae

Compound Eyes

Legs

Mandibles

11

The Life of an Ant

An ant begins its life as a white or yellow egg. This egg is so tiny that it is smaller than a piece of dust! After a few weeks, a small, white worm comes out of the egg. This worm is called a larva.

The legless ant larva is helpless. Worker ants feed and take care of the larva. The larva eats a lot of food and grows. It **sheds** its skin many times as it grows. When a larva stops growing, it turns into a **pupa** and rests. In time, a pupa turns into an adult ant.

These ants are in the resting, or pupal, period before becoming adult ants. The pupa generally looks like a white adult ant.

Setting Up House

A queen ant is a female that is born with wings. When a queen becomes an adult, she flies away from the nest to start a colony of her own. After she finds a male, the two mate. A short time later, the male dies.

The queen then finds or digs a hole in the ground in which to live. She will stay inside her nest the rest of her life, so the queen no longer needs wings. She bites or breaks them off. Then the queen lays eggs in her new nest.

Here worker ants are moving eggs to a new nest. The queen is the large ant on the left.

Lunchtime

The oldest worker ants generally find food for the colony. These ants are called foragers. Forager ants do not live long because they often face enemies and bad weather. They must also carry pieces of food that weigh up to 20 times their body weight.

Most ants eat parts of plants, such as seeds. Some ants eat dead insects or spiders. Certain types of ants drink sweet juice from flowers, called nectar, or tree sap. An ant has four tiny sticks near its mouth called palps. Ants use palps to taste food and push it into their mouth.

Some kinds of ants farm aphids and other nectar-producing bugs. The ants keep the aphids safe from enemies and the aphids let the ants eat their nectar.

Ant Enemies

An ant's biggest enemy is other ants. Ants fight other colonies because they want to win a new nest or more land. In a war between ant colonies, workers from each side will fight to the death. Some colonies have special soldier ants, whose main job is to fight and keep the colony safe.

Ants have little chance of fighting off animals such as frogs, birds, lizards, spiders, and anteaters that hunt them for food. People are also a danger to ants. Some people think ants are a pest and spray them with **insecticides**.

This lizard has its eye on a tasty ant, which it will soon make its lunch. Ants can do little to keep themselves safe from enemies like this.

Living with Ants

Ants are an important part of nature. As they dig and move dirt, they mix air into the soil. This helps plants grow. Ants also move thousands of different plant seeds, which helps these plants spread to new places. Some ants eat small insects that hurt crops. Instead of using insecticides, farmers in China put weaver ants in their fruit tree fields to keep them safe from pests.

While some ants are helpful, others are not. Leafcutter ants take leaves off young fruit trees. Every day they destroy crops valued at **millions** of dollars.

These leafcutter ants live in the Amazon in South America. Leafcutter ants can hurt the trees as they gather leaves to bring back to their nest.

Ants Are Everywhere!

Ants live almost everywhere. You can find them in wet rain forests and dry, sandy deserts. They live on busy city sidewalks and in quiet country fields. The only place you will not find ants is Antarctica. It is cold and snowy there all year.

People who study ants say there are about 10 **quadrillion** ants on Earth! Ants may be small, but their numbers add up. Would you believe the weight of all the ants in the world equals the weight of all the people? We share our Earth with lots of ants!

Glossary

abdomen (AB-duh-mun) The large, back part of an insect's body.

antennae (an-TEH-nee) Thin, rodlike feelers located on the head of certain animals.

compound eyes (KOM-pownd EYZ) The larger eyes of bugs, which are made up of many simple eyes.

exoskeleton (ek-soh-SKEH-leh-tun) The hard covering on the outside of an animal's body that holds and guards the soft insides.

insecticides (in-SEK-tih-sydz) Matter used to kill insects.

insects (IN-sekts) Small animals that often have six legs and wings.

mate (MAYT) To join together to make babies.

millions (MIL-yunz) Thousands of thousands.

picnic (PIK-nik) An outing to which food is brought and eaten outside.

pupa (PYOO-puh) The second stage of life for an insect, in which it changes from a larva to an adult.

quadrillion (kwah-DRIL-yun) A very large number with 15 zeros on the end.

sheds (SHEDZ) Gets rid of an outside covering, like skin.

thorax (THOR-aks) The middle part of the body of an insect. The wings and legs attach to the thorax.

Index

Web Sites

Due to the changing nature of Internet links, PowerKids Press has developed an online list of Web sites related to the subject of this book. This site is updated regularly. Please use this link to access the list:
www.powerkidslinks.com/umbb/ant/